The Rock Island Hiking Club

The Rock Island Hiking Club

Poems by Ray A. Young Bear

UNIVERSITY OF IOWA PRESS Ψ IOWA CITY

University of Iowa Press, Iowa City 52242
Printed in the United States of America
Design by Richard Hendel
http://www.uiowa.edu/~uipress

The publication of this book was generously
supported by the University of Iowa Foundation.

Printed on acid-free paper

Library of Congress
Cataloging-in-Publication Data
Young Bear, Ray A.
The Rock Island Hiking Club: poems / by Ray A.
Young Bear.
p.   cm.
ISBN 0-87745-770-0 (cloth),
ISBN 0-87745-771-9 (pbk.)
1. Indians of North America—Poetry.   2. Fox
Indians—Poetry.   I. Title.

PS3575.0865 R63   2001
811'.54—dc21   00-068025

01 02 03 04 05 C 5 4 3 2 1
01 02 03 04 05 P 5 4 3 2 1

For

Ada Kapayou Old Bear,

Chloe Young Bear,

Stella Lasley Young Bear,

& Grandmother Earth

Contents

Acknowledgments

"The Reptile Decree from Paris" originally appeared in the
Kenyon Review; "The Rock Island Hiking Club" in the *Virginia
Quarterly Review* and the *Wicazo Sha Review*; "The Aura of the Blue
Flower That Is a Goddess" and "January Gifts from the Ground Squirrel
Entity" in *Akwe:kon*; "Summer Tripe Dreams and Concrete Leaves" and
"Father Scarmark—World War I Hero—and Democracy" in *Ploughshares*;
"Our Bird Aegis" in *Callaloo*; "Eagle Feathers in Colour Photocopy" in
Solo; "The Mask of Four Indistinguishable Thunderstorms" in *Witness*;
"The Bread Factory" and "For Lazy-Boys, Devoted Pets, Health, and
Tribal Homeland Reality, or How We Are Each a Lone Hovercraft" in
the *Gettysburg Review*; and "Poems for Dreams and Underwater Portals"
in *Flyway*.

The Rock Island Hiking Club

Symbolically, they stand close together
as they have done throughout their lives
on the Black Eagle Child Settlement. They peer
nervously into the canvas-shaded bigtop where
the tribal celebration is about to take place:
Mary Two Red Foot in her brilliant
cotton-white skirt has her one-year-old,
big-boned grandson, Robert No Body, slung
on her back in a green yarn-fringed shawl.

In the choking humidity, the serrated trim
of the tent vibrates as a concert bass drum
is being tuned. Mary squints in the harsh
daylight and begins talking: *"A kwi ma ka ski
bi ta bi ya ni ni-tte na-ki tta bi wa ki.*
I can't see in there, but they're already
seated." All she can make out are silhouettes
of singers on bales of hay.

Her younger half-sister, Doreen Half Elk,
with unseen hands on hips leans over
and listens intently. In the heat all Doreen
wishes to show is her face. A black-and-gray-
striped shawl covers her body and head.
Even her feet and shoes are in the dark
shade of her ruffled skirt. She's a statue
whose base is the earth.

Beside them, sitting in a semi-circle
on the ground, four white men in neckties,
suspenders, and straw hats are having lunch.
The baby, No Body, looks down at the men
who are nearly transparent in the hot
July 15, 1932, sun.

Our Bird Aegis

An immature black eagle walks assuredly
across a prairie meadow. He pauses in mid-step
with one talon over the wet snow to turn
around and see.

Imprinted in the tall grass behind him
are the shadows of his tracks,
claws instead of talons, the kind
that belong to a massive bear.
And he goes by that name:
Me kwi so ta.

And so this aegis looms against the last
spring blizzard. We discover he's concerned
and the white feathers of his spotted hat
flicker, signaling this.

With outstretched wings he tests the sutures.
Even he is subject to physical wounds and human
tragedy, he tells us.

The eyes of the Bear-King radiate through
the thick, falling snow. He meditates on the loss
of my younger brother—and by custom
suppresses his emotions.

American Flag Dress

You know, my father, Willy Potato, and his cousin,
Jason Scarmark, are known throughout Iowa.
They came back from World War I as highly
decorated heroes. Newspaper clippings
from the *Des Moines Chronicle* were kept
under glass at the Tama County courthouse.
These we were allowed to view once a year
during the field trip taken by Weeping
Willow Elementary. While the courthouse
collections were housed ten miles away,
the tarnished medals and wrinkled ribbons
always had an effect on us even when they
seemed so far away—like stars. Letters
of honor received by the Potato Cousins
were read to us by teachers, and we
were astounded by photographs of how
they smiled with arms interlocked years ago
amid the burning fields, twisted armor, and death.

We were told that when trouble in Northern Europe
resurfaced, the Potato Cousins made news again
for volunteering their services to America.
But the gallant offer was politely denied.
From this unwavering act of courage many
an immigrant heart was stirred. And so when
the teenage sons of white farmers enlisted in
record numbers from the surrounding counties,
the Potato Cousins were credited for instilling
a fervid sense of patriotism.
Once when a journalist asked the cousins what
drove them to defend the country, my father said:
"*A kwi ma-me ta kwi-mi ka ti ya ki ni. I ni-ye to ki-*
a tta wa i-e tta i wa ji-ne me tto e me na na ki.
We do not like to fight. Perhaps this is the way it was
for our grandfathers." The loose

translation was turned around to read:
"We like to fight—unlike our grandfathers."
They were soon in demand at county
celebrations and state fairs.

In exchange for "gas, food, and *no* lodging,"
the heroes would don Sioux, *A tta*, war bonnets
and woolen uniforms to march in parades.
I would accompany them—not having a choice
in the matter— as reigning princess of the Annual
Black Eagle Child Field Days. On the hottest
and most humid summer days I felt sorry
for them as they led the processions in tight
combat boots while the State Pork Queen
and her rosy-cheeked court rode in automobiles.
Myself included, but on the trunk, facing backward.
And following behind would be the King of the Hobos,
an ever-present celebrity. He sat on a tan horse next
to the town mayors and assorted dignitaries.
On the Hobo King's secret signal the half-intoxicated
men would crow like ragged roosters as they looked at
my exposed ankles and chapped shins.

Among them always would be the bald-headed
white prophet named Mark. Well-rounded and portly
in his foul-smelling buckskin and fur hat, Mark
would nervously rub his glistening forehead
by habit and produce toothpick-size rolls
of dirt. These unwanted gifts were tossed
to our feet like ritual before he would say,
"Long before there was Hitler I dreamt
of him, Willy." In disgust my father could
only grimace and joke in Indian to Jason about
the dirt toothpick–manufacturing fat man.
"*Ne ki-me ko-e be ma te si ya ni-a kwi-ko i ye-*

na na tti-ke ke ne ma ki ni-ma ni-ni a bi ji-
wi ne si ji. Mo ko ma na-ke e i ki-ma na!
As long as I've lived never have I known
anyone to be this dirty. And this is a white
person!"

The Black Eagle Child Doughboys were often
billed as the main attraction. The cousins would
march triumphantly to their own unique chant:
"Ma ni tta-ni a ne mi-i tti tti mo ya kwi
Germany *na i na-ma na na kwi!* This is the way
our voices will sound when we attack Germany!"
When the march paused, they expertly removed
the long, gleaming bayonets from their rifles
and placed them in the scabbards without looking.
Then they'd take turns singing war dance songs
for each other on the deerhide drum made from
a quarter of a wooden barrel.

From April to September we traveled
to the cardinal points of Iowa, from Titonka
to Corydon and beyond, camping along
picturesque cliffs of the Mississippi,
or the green rolling banks of the water–
clouded–by–a–fleeing–Culture Hero's–foot
Missouri River. Wearing an American flag
dress I would wave to the crowd with my
red-tailed hawk fan, and I became accustomed
to the ugly, sky-reflecting marble eyes
                    of the white children.
With blond disheveled hair they rolled over
the cobblestone streets mimicking death
from flint-tipped arrows. If they came close
enough where I could actually see my bright
reflection, I'd spit.

In the bizarre pretense we were allied against
a common Teutonic threat, one could say I barely
justified everyone's existence and survivability—
a living, breathing Statue of Liberty. . . .

The Aura of the Blue Flower That Is a Goddess

Immediately after the two brothers entered
the Seafood Shoppe with their wide-eyed wives
and extra-brown complexioned stepchildren,
the shrimp scampi sauce suddenly altered
its taste to bitter dishsoap. It took a moment
to realize the notorious twosome were "carrying"
medicines, and that I was most likely the next
target in the supernatural shooting gallery.
It was yet another stab at my precious
shadow, *ne no ke we ni*, the one who
always Stands First, wildly unafraid
but vulnerable.

This placement of time, this chance meeting
at Long John Silver's, had already been discussed
over the burning flower clusters, approved,
and scheduled for a divine assassination.
What an ideal place to invisibly send forth
a petroglyph thorn to the sensitive
and unsuspecting instep I thought.
Out of fear I had to spit out the masticated
crustacean into the folded Dutch bandanna.
I signaled Selene with my eyes:
something is terribly wrong here.

Even in the old stories, *ke ta-a ji mo na ni*,
my grandmother recited there was always
disagreement, jealousy, and animosity
between supernatural deities. That
actuality for humans, *me to se na ni wa ki*,
however was everpresent. It didn't conclude
as an impasse that gave us the weather,
the four seasons, the stars, sun, and moon.
Everything that was held together.

                    Unfortunately,
there could only be one re-creation
of earth. If it was requested in the aura
of the blue flower that I die,
the aura will make sure I die. . . .

Later, the invisible thorn—when removed by
resident-physicians (paying back their medical
loans)—would transform into some unidentifiable
protoplasm and continue to hide in the more
sensitive, cancer-attracting parts of the fish-
eater.

In the mythical darkness that would follow
the stories the luminescent mantle of the kerosene
lamp would aptly remind me of stars who cooled
down in pre-arranged peace—to quietly wait
and glow.

Father Scarmark—World War I Hero—and Democracy

The black uncombed wig with stiff grotesque braids
sits atop his broad and pockmarked forehead;
and his grip on the dull tomahawk is almost woman-
like. Yes, Father Scarmark's winsome eyes
and slouched spine do not befit a proven warrior.
But the beaded American flag designs on the bayonet
scabbard symbolize breaths stolen from German officers.
Back then he was called Master Check because he made
sure captured officers died mysteriously from minor
wounds during pauses in the artillery fire.

Today Father Scarmark is a chronic worrier; his tears
radiate eerily from the inside corners of his eyes.
He says he can vividly recall trench warfare.
We have been taught to distinguish that each
campaign has its own unique choking emanation.
But we have yet to understand what the Foggy
Dawn revealed: measurements of sanity?
And the eviscerated remains of young,
unsuspecting adversaries? He knows other,
far more gruesome elements, as does his family.
They know the intimate details through the crude
odor that sometimes surfaces from the dilated pores
of his sweaty body.

And the long johns under his old-time dance outfit
are fiery red. In his armpit, almost hidden by
the mirrored arm bustles, is the Bible he helped
translate into our mother tongue. They say
Scarmark's resurrection and pathologic vengeance
began when he was taken prisoner. This was early on.
There are stories he was maimed at parties of the German
echelon. Others say he was kept alive on boiled rats.

Fate arrived one afternoon as he was attempting
suicide. An artillery round landed above the bunker

at the exact moment he hanged himself. In the fiery
dust that followed, as the crudely fashioned noose
locked in tight braid-increments around his neck,
a page from *Tti-tte-sa*, Jesus, floated toward him
like a harmless moth and remained stationary,
long enough for him to read about the criminals
who were nailed beside Christ. Once he begged
for his Forgiveness, the rope loosened itself
and rose mysteriously to the ceiling and burned
in the shape of a crucifix. Although the fire
went out, its ethereal shape was imprinted
in the European air.

Today "Father J. Scarmark"—as his name reads
on the deteriorating mission door—had this phantom
transfiguration painted on the church.
"Ma ni ke-mi ne kwi ya ni-be ma te si we ni.
This is what gave me my life" is the painting's title.
It is marveled at by the few daring white people
who stop at the mission on their sightseeing scurry
through the Settlement.

Although he speaks in repetitions and clichés,
Father Scarmark gets incensed if family members
mock his unoriginality. Under the grotesque black
wig, his family recited, should be stamped
"Boastful War Hero." Yet few in the tribe can
match his deeds. Over supper he is known to say:
"I ni ye to ki-we tti-mi ya ne ne mi ya tti.
E we ta se i ya ni. That is probably the reason
they are jealous of me. Since I am a proven
veteran. *A kwi ke-e ma ma to mo na ni we ya ni.*
And not because I am a religious man."
But the male heirs knew differently.
Especially Scarmark the Second.

"Bravery in war has nothing to do with it,"
he once told his brothers, who always
held his judgments in reserve.
But he went on and they listened
to the shrewd history of Black Eagle Child
politics: it was their father who formed
the 1923 Business Council after tampering
with the ballot boxes. At issue was democracy—
the one-person, one-vote concept. Unfortunately,
their father's father had raped and murdered
a young woman, Dorothy Black Heron;
and the county authorities offered to forget
the crime if the Scarmark patriarch agreed
to become a federally recognized Chief
and allow education into the tribe.
When their father saw his father step
perfectly into his own moccasin tracks,
at the scene, there was no choice but
to burn the pivotal vote.

From there on out, American Indians
as practicing Democrats and Republicans
became a literal myth. That single,
incinerated vote, as would be seen by scholars
later on, initiated the arduous rock-strewn
journey toward our demise. Every jagged edge
stabbed our sensitive feet and we became
hobble-legged. Mandatory education
for tribal youth was enacted by the state
of Iowa at the expense of "Heron, Dorothy Black."
Often their father would openly reflect (long before
the sons could fathom the implications of the story)
that had the election swung for sacred, traditional
chieftainship the "Cigarstore Indian" days
would have returned. It was well known most

youth fled to the hills in short-lived protest.
When food and water supplies were depleted
they came out to federal truant officers
who patiently herded them to the barn stalls
for the wicked and cultural disfiguring.

The Reptile Decree from Paris

What could my one-armed grandfather, Victor Bearchild,
possibly be presenting to the Caucasian visitor
named Subchief? (In elementary I used thick
ugly tablets by that same name.) It doesn't look
like any kind of "Trophy" as the label notes.
It's not a silver-plated rendition
of basketball players or runners in miniature
on the fireplace mantel. First appearances
through the magnifying glass indicate
the speckled hide of some animal,
covering the visitor's pale hand
and Victor's sleeve-knotted half arm;
and in the blurred background is a maple
sapling in front of a whitewashed house.
A closer look reveals the open beak
of a predator bird whose wingfeathers
have been trimmed into spikes, with serrated
edges. Several loose feathers are entwined
around the uncommon combination
of the animal-bird's torso.

In my grandfather's good left hand
is a paper document that has been folded
so much sections hang on weakly by creased
corners only. Can we zoom in on his "left"
and then down? In front of his hefty shoes
is a tin box—approximately eight by ten inches—
where important items were stored.
The bird's screaming face and its
speckled ally must have protected
the contents with supernaturalism
from those curious enough to pry.
And there would be loose stones
that rattled and rumbled against the walls

of the box like distant earth tremors,
a mystical alarm that woke both owner
and sentinel.

My Woodlands people, having adopted
the alphabet in the 1600s, often kept
communiqués from Great Britain, Spain,
and France. These mats or "scrolls"
were considered valuable expressions
of other "Man," and tribal keepers
passed these indecipherable symbols
from one generation to the next.
Some contained signatures of distant
Kings and Queens, including their wax seals
and ribbons. If the scroll had a story that
could be remembered as having a history-making
role where sacred aid was conjured, it became
part of the clan altar.

In the 1930s, however, when anthropologists
were allowed to translate one scroll
we were apprised it was a decree from
a King in Paris, ordering our "total
extermination. Leave not a single limb
intact, for this race can regenerate
itself back to life like reptiles."
Why? the elders expressed meekly.
Because the trading toll your grandfathers
demanded from tribes and foreigners
passing through your territories,
related Dr. Culsax in the kerosene-lit
interior of the earth lodge, was deemed
"unreasonable and highly insulting."
The Reptile Decree eventually drove us
south from Wisconsin into Illinois,

then Kansas in exile, and finally here—
to Iowa.

Jesus, this photo could be that very scroll!
It's not any prize then.
With that as confirmation I begin to align
the sunlight through the glass and burn
minute holes in the emulsion and grain,
hoping the fiery light will reach
the jewel-clustered fingers
of ancient royalty, transgressing
time: someone's offensive decision.
I wholly deny and retract all prayers
it listened to and received in error—
centuries of misery. Joseph Campbell,
punch "Esc." The software of mythologic
understanding dissolves.

Looking again I notice the knee portion
of my grandfather's trousers bulging out,
even as he stands erect. The imprint
of his kneecaps is solid, like evidence
of—too much sitting? But he's middle-aged,
and he was never idle. Hell, he was a bloody
wood-carver! (The "phantom knee" effect
is a tribal term which refers to clothes
that accumulate dirt and grease from constant wear.
The joke being, the clothes will come to life
whenever the ignorant owner decides to take
them off. The mere association embarrasses me.
My own grandfather, of all people.)
It isn't that he was too lazy to dress for company;
it is probably because he only had two pairs
of trousers. Of course. And there was no
laundry soap that week in 1934 when the bird-

animal entity was rudely awakened by the harsh
sunlight—without ample warning from stones,
or an earth tremor. No appointment was made,
Dear Charlevoix.

January Gifts from the Ground Squirrel Entity

It can go beyond the case of wild, little animals
storing dozens of Black Eagle Child beans and acorns
(two sizes) in conspicuous places throughout the trailer.
Winter is an impetus, obviously, but there's a strong
suspicion that the beans and acorns found between
our towels, clothes, and footwear are gifts
from deities who reside on this pinetree-lined
hillside. Since they cannot reveal themselves,
they probably appointed these intermediaries.
But the fact there are no fields or forests
that would bear these particular varieties
within a quarter-mile circumference makes
a sane and logical argument against ground
squirrels or mice making the storage trek
in a single night.

Before the performance trip to St. Mary's College
in Winona, Minnesota, I found eight shiny acorns
in my Reebok tennis shoes, the pair I would have worn
for driving, not the ones I use under theatre lights.
It was definite I'd use them. And Selene found
gray, brittle ones in her sewing machine, in compart-
ments that could not have been opened by any creature.
Strangely, the year before that, before leaving for Taos,
our favorite wine glasses were filled to the brim
with beans called *bi ya*.

I've also theorized the gifts are paybacks
from grateful chipmunks who grew fat last summer
on commodity surplus peanuts, the ones I fed them
as they appeared on the log pile in the yard,
facing the earthlight for the first time
with miniature black eyes. But all is contradicted
by the memory of a Grandfather who owned a tin
antique suitcase filled mysteriously with acorns

he said must have been brought by mice.
No one ever had the audacity to ask:
How could they gnaw through metal?

And just recently when I saw walnuts fall
from an overhanging oak limb and land precisely
in the four corners of a satin-lined casket
of the woman I was paying my respects to,
I had to rethink the whole scenario.
There was my blind uncle, you see,
in the dream about "The Bread Factory"
that came to mind.

The Mask of Four Indistinguishable Thunderstorms

It is the thunderstorm
        at first
that begins speaking
        from an easterly direction
We listen to its vociferous
        non-threatening
voice and fall asleep

This weather doesn't care
        to know itself
our inner physical journals
record

We assess: icy rain is no different
        than wet branch-breaking
snow and the summer deluge
        that stretches
toward autumn combines all into one
        haunting answer

That of a wintry inevitability
        glazed ice
over the terrain
        The symphony

Before awakening we hear clouds
that quietly explode
        from within
Watery moonlit fragments hit
        the roof
        saying: in the case of anger
fist-sized hail would splinter
        everything

The woodlands horizon
is therefore portrayed as a jagged
        lavender line

and encircled in yellow
                    obviously
is the sun
            reducing humankind
to spherical dimensions
                    making
known the presence
of duality

That the Black Hummingbirds
are saviours as well as
assassins

                    / / /

Grandmother Earth
sits with her bare razor-nicked
back toward you
                    the observer
the would-be infringer
            the one who taps out
salvation messages with a silver
surgical instrument

Her daughter's precious son
            she recognizes
But the blood-letting is deceptive
What was supposed
                    to be seasonal
self-purification appears through
            ultrasound
as a protoplasmic thorn
carved with indecipherable
                    petroglyphs

                    / / /

We swear nothing is apocalyptic
while garish beacons from
        the tribal gaming complex
create apparitions
in the sky

Balanced on a floating mass
        of ourselves and
under the guidance of an ochre
                seal-eyed
word-collector in a tight
flannel shirt
        hole-ridden jeans
and Presbyterian church–donated
        shoes
we cradle fine shovels
that are designed to slice
        the earth
leaving behind rectangular-
        shaped markings
of a former industrious
society

Summer Tripe Dreams and Concrete Leaves

I.

There exists a future when green trees will be extinct.
In our ingenuity artificial tree factories—ATFS—
     will flourish.

Far ahead I see myself walking under one,
and I grow uneasy at the thought of chunks
of painted concrete swaying in the man-made
breeze from bark-textured iron rods.

Don't worry, says the regional safety inspector,
they can withstand mega-knot winds.
Plus they've got internal warning mechanisms
with stress signals linked to monolithic fans
in the western part of the state. Should a fracture
occur, the fans are automatically programmed
to slow down.

Bullshit, I think as white dust and chips
of paint blow about in the false wind,
stippling my indolent face.

2.

Inside the honeycomb-lined tripe intestine
there is a woman held captive, and I am there with her.

She resembles Debra Winger, the Hollywood actress.
She sits on my lap undressed and allows me to explore
her smooth virginal skin, her sensuousness.
Outside of her bone frame and beyond the newborn,
translucent skin, she cries. Together we hear herself.

The fine design on the walls and the terraced floors
begin to tremble. One end of the floor begins to surge
like an ocean wave and it travels beneath—
and lifts us upward, speeding toward
consciousness.

Eagle Feathers in Colour Photocopy

Edgar Bearchild uses modern non-electric tools
to make duplicates of his grandfather's feather boxes,
and while he can find 1920s-style jewelry
and brass mirror cases at flea markets for decorative
                   inlay, the museums by law
can only buy eagle feathers in colour photocopy,
for the American symbol for freedom faces
extinction. Again. So before setting out on
Interstate 35 north to St. Euripides,
               Edgar places these facsimiles
in the hollowed-out portion of oblong board
and treats them as his predecessors did, keeping
them enclosed and therefore dry between lightweight
wood until the moment needed in either Black Eagle
           Child prayer, combat, or sorcery.

"They almost look real . . . if you look real close,
squinting one eye," comments the Asian-looking
curator with the faux Armani suit and butch
haircut. Edgar thinks a proper reply might entice
             a sale, but he panics
in not knowing the curator's gender. He pops
the brass compact open and sees the two of them
in the mirror, together. One androgynous, the other
with hope. *Neither of us, because of our slender-*
            shaped eyes, really
has to squint that much, was what he wanted
to say. The curator and a tribal staff member
wink at each other. Only then the Gothic
eyeshade. She nods, winces in cancerous
            agreement, and dictates:
"Ethnoforms Project: Black Eagle Child
Featherbox Maker, Edgar Bearchild of Central
Iowa, entitled, 'No. 4029, My Summer at Fortune
Lodge, Alaska.'"

Like a capricious judge at a cattle show that
had just slapped his rear with a blue ribbon,
Ed's rear shinnied. "Why Fortune, and did
you go there?" she asked. I once sensed
                    a murderer there,
or its Anchorage victim knew something about
that place. Her Leica eyes mechanically blinked,
urging him to elaborate. He held up the lid
of the wooden box: covered under
        beveled glass, matboard,
and brass screws, a 4 by 16 inch relief
sculpture on catlinite of a pointy-eared dog
knelt Sphinx-like at the end of a pipestem.
"$4,029.00, and the flute-pipe is included?"
        Yes, twice. This blindfolded
figure on the Lazy-Boy is a self-portrait.
Over the keys my fingers are held in musical
suspension, while the Swirling Red Arrow
is gourd-rattle conceived. Assessing
                    events quickly, the arrow
draws a blue, wavy horizon, like that
ocean where the killer whale swims,
half-surfacing. Thus, within its faraway body
names, addresses, letters, and numbers
        are delineated. And only that.
Behind the dog's neck swirls of smoke
are being emitted from the bowl of the pipe,
Sherlock Holmes that I am.

The Bread Factory

The tribal bread factory is missing,
as well as the pigfeet-canning operation.
And the light-complexioned, physically
challenged woman, the one who controlled
the giant stainless steel tumbler, knows why.
Mystery solver that Lisa Jean is.

Above, over the green rounded hill,
my catatonic uncle strikes the partially
embedded walnuts with his hooked cane.
This is a testament, he reports, to the stars
that fell overnight in legions. Like large
chunks of hail that have just landed,
the walnuts pop up and roll away.

Lured by indiscernible words
I follow behind meekly, a servant
about to be entombed. In my hand
a dark wooden bowl. Beneath the greasy
dish towel there are more walnuts and many
are cracked, dusty, and dry. (Later, through
the Ground Squirrel, there would be acorns.)

"So wha' 'bout your dream-ma 'bout paranormal
golf?" complained the mystery-solving woman.
With clinking leg braces and crutches she
hobbled toward me. In a breath of vanilla
extract and worry she said, "Mine dealt with a water-
less aquarium filled with newborn ground hogs.
An educator then advised me to pour in a half
cup of water to prolong their life."

Beside her tall sister, Lisa Jean kneaded
the dough over the flour-covered table.
Wrists she slashed every summer were visible.
When the raised scar tissue was accidentally

brushed, an eyelid tick ensued. As she leaned
forward in her beige flower print dress,
engrossing herself in work, I visualized
a shameful thought—a phantasmagoric
union between us. Long elegant legs
in black knit socks behind splints
of chrome steel. . . .

A Season of Provocations and Other Ethnic Dreams

1.

It began near the site
of a smoldering but vacant
mobile home. East Quail
Road. There, blared the scanner,
relatives conveyed a teenager
was upset for being deprived
of a "real Three Stooges
videotape." Thus was the sky
ignited. Next, through the jet's
window, I waved to my wife,
Selene Buffalo Husband,
as the bus-like craft turned
over a runway of corn stalk
stumps. And then we ascended,
westward. Unbuckled, I sat in
the back and stretched my arms
across the tops of a soft bench.
Standing beside me, an ethnic
pilot was uneasy. He deflected
my questions with stares toward
earth of concern. Like an amateur
verbal boxer I recited: "Best to leave
a rock that refuses to talk alone;
best just to listen to the water
rippling around it."

2.

Once, after an all-night drive
to Taos, New Mexico, I became
disoriented. At some plaza square,
perhaps close to the designated

meeting place with the poetry
reading contact, I approached
a group of ethnics on a balcony
and, thinking they were other
invited poets, asked: "Are you
here to meet Peter Cottontail?"
Unflinchingly, while wiping salad
bits from their mouths, they pointed
to each other. "No, but we have Bugs
Bunny here—and, oh, here's Daffy!"
Travel-faced in their expensive sun-
glasses I was convex at the ethnologic
query about who I was. Sí, I said, an
Indio, from a nearly immiscible history.
Years later, I recall this exchange
and wonder if Woody Woodpecker
really has a daughter and what
her name might be. Is it Splinter?
you knothead. Methinks it's a clue
from Oklahoma via the Lazy-Boy
quest sessions in the disappearances
of Lauria and Ashley.

3.

English for Black Eagle Childs,
Pat "Dirty" Red Hat once noted,
is saturated with linguistic pitfalls.
For example, he once asked
a coy waitress at an old German-
style restaurant on Interstate 80,
"Do you serve alcoholics?"
"Yes, we do," he was told
that Sunday morning. At a Sears

auto garage the manager peace-
signed when Pat asked about
"hallucinogenic" rather than
halogen headlights. And at
the Youth Services Facility
co-workers oft-reflected when
he "applied a Heineken" on
a muskmelon pulp-choking
girl. That singular misapplication
had more notice than the turbulent
adolescence saved. But no one quipped
at the line given when he mis-dressed
himself: "I am completely reverse
of what I am." Because that term
could fit anyone, ethnic—
or otherwise.

For Lazy-Boys, Devoted Pets, Health, and Tribal Homeland Reality, or How We Are Each a Lone Hovercraft

Deceived by
autumn dust
movement that would've
brushed daylight
from the Lazy-Boy
was expended
needlessly

*

Polar Bear
"the Nicole S. Special"
aligns its Akita profile
in the small clear
spot on the window
where frost has been
scraped
reminding me
that even *he*
is important
as "Won-ton"
my fiction(al)
editor

*

Life I like
said my brain
to its unabashed
self but a back-
ache? *No* re-
sounded a reply
that set off

from within
a soundless
fire alarm fashioned
from sculpture
remnants
of pulsating
nerve endings
making Milky
Way the after-
flash of the
Creator's blink
throughout my
universal
physicality

*

Bear your letters
fish without eyes
drift in currents
embedded in soil

Crows are tossed
in black clusters
by the windshield
wipers

*

Every morning
this spring is without
my younger brother's
massiveness

No red wagon
with three round-
faced children coming up
the muddy driveway
nearly toppling

No massiveness
No eternity
in 1995

Poems for Dreams and Underwater Portals

1.

Behind Selene and Javier Buffalo Husband
the wooded river valley emits a resilient
green-yellow glow. From earth's
supernatural seam bubbles in twin
forms surface, erasing with their color
of eminence that transfixed sense
called Normalcy.

2.

Quiet singing summer,
quiet singing summer.

Within the swan dance
formation, though, two
with young are not typical.
Especially when one
newborn refuses to release
the cut-beaded handle
of a fan. Hers. Then
the green snow cone
becomes an issue.

Like an accident-bound
train, the dancers brake
and collect themselves
in a timely sigh. When
the drum's rumble—
a signal—is softened,
they go backward.
Summer singing
quietly.

3.

Without legs the elongated,
round back of a wooden chair
rests in a ditch. Discarded.
Next, a young woman wearing
a yellow house-cleaning glove that
is vertical appears. Before the corner
of a star quilt lands perfectly in my palm,
waking me, I hoist my arm like a flag:
Was that Ashley Judd?

4.

Through certain readings
of old documents that visually
self-translate, we influence the sunlight
to assume triangle-shaped machinations.
Here the purple ink is Animistic.
Over the wind-trampled prairie grass
where the small lodges glistened
under the all-sky flashes,
we sang: Risk. Risk. And then
two more for assurance
in a non-human domain.

November 12, 1951

"Literary expression,"
Edgar Bearchild once noted,
"is a sadistic mutation of the genes
of intelligence—on my father's side—
that I was unjustly deprived of."

Improvised Sealant for Hissing Wounds

Crumpled clothes on a Lazy-Boy
recliner. This chair is the source
that shapes vague or distinct
pictures behind my smoky
blindfolded eyes. But there
are other things, too, like a basin
plug that clicks and attracts
me to its trademark: "Alley."
So now this is a phantasm,
forming beyond cedar-shadow,
a visitor—a summation
for the Navigator.

In a room beset with faint light:
A jogging suit, baseball cap,
sunglasses, and Dr. Crockston
who's under sedation for
keeping a secret via slow
death by alcohol.

There's no space in his
physiology to make amends
to Facepaint who died from
complications of sharpened
screwdrivers. "The Doc" was
there with the first Black Eagle
Child Settlement cross-dressers.
In his raspy breathing I sense
a conspiracy coming
through the duct tape
sarcophagus: He, too,
will become a mute,
inaccessible shadow
unless the significance
of "15 air waves
tickets" can be deciphered.

An Act of Purification, No. 1

"Normalcy," wrote Bearchild
in *The Black Eagle Child Journals*,
"is an acquisition that dresses
itself in rigorous yet unassailable
forms of temerity." But when
the tall metal ladder covered
itself with a cross child's frosty
handprints, the Recall petition
for one *bo ki te ba* or hole-in-
the-head was promptly cleansed
with braided strips of smoky,
ethnobotanic persuasion. There
was, after all, the lunatic social
worker who preyed on troubled
clientele at tribal cemeteries and
a brother whose house had been
lightning-struck, setting fire to
stolen casino surveillance equipment.
And everything began "with a talking
Go-Kart . . ."

Four Poems for Immediacy

1.

Selene Nicotine of Pinelodge Lake
forms herself from the icy night winds.
With hummingbird-like appendage
borrowed from a moth, her surfboard
is invisible.

Floating beside me I detect her
mythic scent, that of a reddish
orange flower, the pollen of which
coats her normal shoes, her
delicate underwings.

As a serpentine hold-out
I intermingle and then recoil
over the stippled concrete.
No one, I later whisper in
the daylight, shall hold anyone
accountable for the first case
of infidelity.

2.

In front of a house with
large windows a whirlwind
lifts while three others align
themselves to the west
in varying heights of descent,
waiting. Like a chiropractor,
my father adjusts to correctness
his face and torso, then steps
outside with an elder to beseech
the fury to calm. Under the closet
frame I clutch an unknown

baby and wince at the banging
wall, at the clenched fist
of a cookie called Massacre.

3.

Englebert Hubberdee,
the hound dog, relays
a thought as I close my
eyes beside the snowy
riverbank: Larger than
a pile of trash bags
there was a figure here.
We scan the tousled area.
Dry grass and deer bones,
oily mud over the frozen
earth, and ghostly fish
resonations.

4.

From under water a pair
of bright animal eyes glows.
Are you—am I right—
a divine sentry? Is this hole
in the tree a door to your
home? The answer
all along is your own:
A Supernatural owns
the submerged rat terrier,
within the phantasmagoric
tree they reside.

Crestwood School of Social Research

1.

Perched high atop the neon-outlined
towers of Crestwood's Rural Cooperative
the giant farm animal faces made
of chrome shimmer. Some, like the swans
and the llamas, are sculpted in German silver.
Depicted in their twisted torsos are their
commercial histories — of sleek hood
ornaments and ochre-stained sacrificial
offerings. Elaborate, they rotate like weather
vanes. Beside them, the Chance Rooster
           Neal breeds of Blue Heelers
are honored, along with the Francine
Choo-Choos and Spike Rusty Mow Mows.
Calibrated to perform every 35 minutes,
the town's notables resemble grotesques.
Displayed along the narrow Crew-C-Fix
Highway, their kinetic shadows stretch,
drifting across small valleys where the gravel,
another success factor, is chalky and lung-
abusive.

2.

As soon as tired eyes close, the air festers
with heinous intent. It's undeniable, so attests
the Swirling Red Arrow ally who motions *ghosts
relive horrific deaths here*. Within its restless
citizens they manifest themselves through eyes
that are silver and reflective, which divide them
into other personalities. From the recesses
of the famous gravel pits, the stories record,

shadow-swallowing serpents once possessed
         flags of Lost Nations.
Who owns who? thus sing the tan deities
of today as a warning—for you to surrender.
That's why their rattles replicate deathly whispers.
Whereas for us it was diamonds, hedonistic
occurrences within God's musical instruments.

3.

Disguised as a gravel pit and encircled by metallic
pendants strung on telephone wire—ten by twenty
square miles—visible only from the sky, the extra-
terrestrial processing station makes this place
ingenuous. For their road lost—it happens
to them, too—the fencepost signs give direction:
O-SO-E-Z reads the first; 2-B-B-Z the second;
SO GET LOST the third; and w/YR AUNT'S
FARM MILK the last.

Closer to the outskirts, Daizy, the Muddi Kow,
winks when her blue milk fills, vacates, and refills
her clear udders. Regular travelers exit I-35
to behold another vacation check-off:
As the electrolyte drains, her long rubber
eyelashes shake. Equally famous, the blue
butter impregnated with yellow cheese dots
is shipped worldwide. "Sticks of Blue, Packed
by Sue." Wearing a Dutch fisherman's cap,
         the Campbell Soupish model
waves its windmill arms to no one. Thereby
creating an access for mythic trickery, I think.
Not even a smelly animal's foot would deter
its quest to restore its vision, using the gray

corneas, the ones taken from you in a crude
ophthalmic surgery. No telltale forensic dye
would imply that the nerve-ending
was severely severed.

4.

After curious motorcycles roar by, I am wrapped
with green inquisitive stripes of light. "The King
of Spain," a lover of Old Bikes, would've delighted
at these contraptions of extreme synergism. For
this month only we are 59 years old. Our grand-
mothers raised us, so the revving of the engines
of the Ram-shaped Cruizers only saddens me.
To Thyself: Not even the monolithic fans
bringing the autumn breeze interest me.
                 Starting from Ida Grove,
near the Buffalo Compounds, I began
missing Selene. Wedged against a Quick-Gal
(lon) bathroom corner and with the .380
Beretta unholstered, this is what I torment:
Tomorrow we'll argue over Nouns & Verbiage,
yes, delaying lessons on Cru-Cials & Other Necess's.
They're scheduled to integrate in one year? So I'm
humored in Morose Levels, crowned racks of it.
Sauteed in sausage grease with snow peas,
mushrooms, ginger, soy sauce, and scallions
manyfold, these venison strips contain
nostalgic protein, memories from
the succulent spine. A soft touch
to the elbow of a dream.

Dish Shapes and Remnant Pools

High above, behind
the extended wings
of cranes, lavender
clouds flatten themselves
into a dish-shaped flotilla.
Heading East, they keep
one cautious space apart.
They would be useful,
I resolve, if they made
the mass of our anxieties
a less orderly horizon.

"That's what's coming,"
I voice-note. "Quick days—
remnant pools of floods,
reflecting indiscernible
choices." Suddenly,
the blue sky scrapes
itself against the forest
canopy of thorns.
From this contact,
premeditated, a giant
cottonwood fluff drifts
toward me crosswind.
Midway North, as if
in dream, a bubble-shape
alights near an uprooted
Box Elder. And then, acting
unwanted, the capricious
sphere rolls into the sweet-
smelling frost.

With the daylight disabled
and mending itself, a *realm-
slipping* event self-manifests:

In former juvenile hands, my
grandfathers' ledgers, which
were written in purple ink,
self-translate from tribal
syllabics to English. To read
inscription without knowing
equals the point where night
introduces daybreak through
the ecstatic songs of circling
geese. Before ruffling their
feathers in furtive ritual,
small swimmers gather
near the green, hollow
stem to re-define themselves.
Everyone dry-mud prepares
for this sensual elaboration,
this moment before autumn,
winter, You, memory-maker,
and the other seasons are issued
from the green, hollow stem—
a flute, as an eagle's
sequential whistles.

In the Tree's Shadow

My dog is as old as my bereavement.
The wooden red wagon dissolves
into the mossy ground. "Madnesse."

A one-cloud rain. Like wild architects
we seed the rough hill with grass.
By machine and wind, trees have fallen.

In the tree's shadow an orange light
holds the sunset's color. I don't question
this Animistic reaching. Of the growth
on the bark that shines.

Moon-like Craters on My Legs

Throughout my investiture
as a "word collector," there
were extraterrestrials disguised
as well-meaning Scandinavians.
You'd think they would've told
me. Stuff I should've known
about or expected, like rat-claw
messages on doors and other
supernatural revealings.

Except for a couple
of visits, there was
never any unfolding,
no alien-to-human
communiqués,
nothing to comport
their omnipresence
except suspected
implant movement.
"Twice, subepidermal
bullet-shaped devices
readjusted on forearms
for reception," I wrote.
"The side-effects consist
of physical extrusions,
like unhealing wounds
or toenails coming off,
regenerating."

Based on which body part
is most susceptible to injury,
the implants calculate where
to skin surface. Rash outbreaks
thus riddle my thighs with scar
tissue, confusing my Specialist.

"Periscopes," I tried to joke.
Finally, with fresh tissue
depleted, they relocated,
taking refuge in my toes.
At the slightest shoe
discomfort or a sun
deck sliver, the feet
suffer.

At least the podiatrist
watches *X-Files* something.
"In a swimming pool once,"
he lets me convey,
"I scraped my knee:
Via antibiotic bandages
the wound could hardly
recoup." Liquid immersion
interfered? "Yes." Chlorine?
"In Albuquerque." He listens
with keen indifference
as I recount our metabolic
and intuitive natures.
"But showers also
provide access to distant
acts of sexual depravity,
like that time I received
the Yosemite killer's
license plate letters
before his last life-
taking."

Another time, I ascertain,
in a drunken hallway scuffle
between lovers I got shin-kicked.
Accidentally. The device

reversed into the bone.
"There, the scar is crescent-
shaped and indented like moon
craters."

Laramie's Peripheral Vision

I.

Small, graceful hawks whose tailfeathers
are decorated with menacing upside-down
faces of ancient swordsmen hunt over
the green, wooded hillside.

A house, symbolically ours, is scheduled
to be built there, we're told — once politics
quell. Whenever that happens, we reply,
the tribal housing contract stipulates we'd
be mere "occupants." Maybe when Laramie
            gets out, offers the mother,
it'll be done? The father raped the tropical
stepdaughter. And that accounts for everything —
right? The world is pockmarked with holes,
son, like the dozens in your dad's freaking
head, King of the Coconuts.

It isn't an impediment, Selene
and I rationalize quietly, occupying
a casino-funded edifice. The sunlit window,
after all, will be the same. The door knobs,
however, will need replacing, likewise
the kitchen cabinets, air ducts,
            closet doors, ceiling,
and the water heater. If the unsealed
foundation doesn't crack, the frame may
last fifty years. So the oxymoron of having
waited five centuries for exclusive non-
ownership of a new house is tolerable. But
think of our patrilineal customs, now tribal
by-laws that preclude women from such
benefits. Nothing — it seems — can ever be
reversed. But there's compromise. And
even precepts are subject to change,

times when they seemingly are no longer
tenable.

2.

To make it free from negativity
this paradoxical house will be blessed
by my father. Later, it'll be swept
for electronic bugs. Even after their
petition-ouster, the relics (rogue tribal
council operatives) remain bothersome.
                    Their relatives now
stalk us, leaving hell's postcards—flares,
in our mailbox. For truckers' showers,
piglet farms, and stock car losers,
tribal sovereignty was waived. (If the Lazy-
Boy Navigator saw deceased relatives change
into geese, wrapping their necks around
the poles of the cosmic earth lodge,
arranging themselves into a message
on how to remove them, politically,
then it was necessary.)

Under "relic" reign, their mish-mash
consultants all named Lowell & Lowell
abated tribal direction. These Pathetics
wore unkempt silver feather earrings,
black dusters, and platinum toupees.
At the VIP rodeo section, they all
ate cups of chilled fruit topped with
whipped cream and arena dust.

Casino-obsessed, they also allowed
trespassers to kill the team-hunting hawks
rather than intervene, evicting them. And

when their own relatives' eyes began
missing the daylight, they were still
             stupid. The Deities,
it was theorized, disagreed with hypocrisy.
There's irony when Priests pray that any
Evil that's directed toward tribal homeland
Pogo-reverse itself. Sitting beside them,
the necro-verted tribal officials, their
own sons, vowing unsuccessfully
to avenge their perceived genetic
deficiencies. In sabotaging tribal
affairs, was it simply because
your Chihuahua relative
bedded their spouse-to-be
before mold with a single hair
grew on its inconspicuous nose?

3.

These empty but jet-streaked clouds
possess details of Laramie's metamorphosis
into a fatherless guitarist. Like the First Earth,
there's transgression and then consequence.
He'll awake, digesting a wide dispersal
of pernicious space. And he'll ask, as would
another, about the purpose of treeless valleys.
Maybe it'll be good, we predict holding Merlots,
him, undergoing therapy. (I knew my father
at ten; he lost his at thirteen. We are what, what
are we to each other—then?) Upon returning,
his petulant sisters will ignore their mother's
call over Rolling Head Valley. A resident-
shadow will flicker in his peripheral vision,
reminding him of Weeping Willow's

Halloween supplies: Court exhibit
photos of Wal-Mart bags crammed
into his closet, some with lollipop
handles sticking out, including
orange edible flutes and candy corn—
next to the poster of Traci Lords,
pre–*Melrose Place*, and purple
Reebok tennis shoes.

4.

On windy days, the hawks agree to catch
invisible currents, spiraling upward until
they vanish in the afterburn-streaked skies.
            Self-assessment is triggered:
That's how I am sometimes. The group task
set aside, like a mortuary custom that doesn't
belong or is poorly conceived. The hawks
will leave to survive, whereas my morbid
victimization thrives. Soon, I expect Caterpillars
to scoop out the reddish brown sand. Above
this hollowed-out hillside, I whisper to Selene,
is where we'll recoup the sound of silverware
clinking against dishes, children's laughter,
life discussion, and where the furniture goes.
My last breath is therefore irrelevant.
Inasmuch as my grandmother took
care of me, including others,
I'll seek the same.